GRIDIRON GREATS

HEROES OF FOOTBALL

JENNIFER RIVKIN

CRABTREE
Publishing Company
www.crabtreebooks.com

FOOTBALL SOURCE

Author: Jennifer Rivkin

Editors: Marcia Abramson, Petrice Custance

Photo research: Melissa McClellan

Design: T.J. Choleva

Cover design: Samara Parent

Proofreader: Janine Deschenes

Editorial director: Kathy Middleton

Prepress technician: Samara Parent

Print coordinator: Margaret Amy Salter

Consultant: R Ian Smith. President.
Ontario Football Alliance

Production coordinated by BlueAppleWorks Inc.

Cover images: Quarterback Johnny Unitas
(Baltimore Colts), fullback Jim Brown (Cleveland
Browns), quarterback Russell Wilson (Seattle
Seahawks), Jennifer Welter coach (Arizona
Cardinals)

Title page image: QB Russell Wilson celebrates
Seattle Seahawks' Super Bowl XLVIII victory

Photographs
Cover: Public Domain (top left); Associated Press: © AP Photo/Elaine Thompson
(top right); © Cal Sport Media via AP Images (bottom right); © AP Photo/NFL
Photos (bottom left)
Interior: Corbis: © Blake Sell/Reuters/Corbis (p 8 left);Shutterstock.com: © dean
bertoncelj (title page);© wavebreakmedia (TOC); pbombaert (page numbers);
© Steve Broer (TOC background); Alexey Stiop (p 5 top); Steve Broer (p 8–9 top);
Joseph Sohm (p 8 bottom); Carlos E. Santa Maria (football); Alexey Stiop (p 12–13
top, 16–17 bottom, 28–29 bottom); Eric Broder Van Dyke (p 12–13 bottom, 28–29 top);
Christopher Penler (p 16–17 top); Keystone Press: © Hector Acevedo (p 9 left); ©
Christopher Szagola(p 10, 13 right, 15, 18, 24, 25); © John Pyle (p 11); © Bob Larson
(p 12 left); © Chicago Tribune (p 16); © George Holland (p 17); © Jacob Paulsen
(p 19); © Erik Williams (p 21); © Tim Warner (p 22); © Jacob Kupferman (p 23);
© Mark Cornelison (p 27 left); © Duncan Williams (p 28); © Craig Lassig (p 29 left);
© Chris Lee (p 29 right); © Michael Prengler (p 30); ZUMAPRESS.com: © Kostas
Lymperopoulos (p 14); © Chris Szagola (p 20); Public Domain: p 6; p 7; Sgt. Johnny
J. Angelo, MN National Guard (p 27 right); Creative Commons: andrewtat94 (title
page middle); Larry Maurer (p 4); Photofest: p 26

Library and Archives Canada Cataloguing in Publication

Rivkin, Jennifer, author
    Gridiron greats : heroes of football / Jennifer Rivkin.

(Football source)
Includes index.
Issued in print and electronic formats.
ISBN 978-0-7787-2295-3 (bound).--ISBN 978-0-7787-2301-1
(paperback).--ISBN 978-1-4271-1730-4 (html)

    1. Football players--Biography--Juvenile literature.
I. Title.

GV939.A1R58 2016   j796.332092'2   C2015-907470-3
    C2015-907471-1

Library of Congress Cataloging-in-Publication Data

Names: Rivkin, Jennifer, author.
Title: Gridiron greats : heroes of football / Jennifer Rivkin.
Description: New York : Crabtree Publishing Company, [2016] | Series:
  Football Source | Includes index. | Description based on print version
  record and CIP data provided by publisher; resource not viewed.
Identifiers: LCCN 2015047161 (print) | LCCN 2015042514 (ebook) | ISBN
  9781427117304 (electronic HTML) | ISBN 9780778722953 (reinforced library
  binding : alk. paper) | ISBN 9780778723011 (paperback : alk. paper)
Subjects: LCSH: Football players--United States--Rating of--Juvenile
  literature.
Classification: LCC GV939.A1 (print) | LCC GV939.A1 R58 2016 (ebook) | DDC
  796.3320922--dc23
LC record available at http://lccn.loc.gov/2015047161

Crabtree Publishing Company
www.crabtreebooks.com   1-800-387-7650

Printed in Canada/012016/BF20151123

Published in Canada
Crabtree Publishing
616 Welland Ave.
St. Catharines, ON
L2M 5V6

Published in the United States
Crabtree Publishing
PMB 59051
350 Fifth Avenue, 59th Floor
New York, New York 10118

Published in the United Kingdom
Crabtree Publishing
Maritime House
Basin Road North, Hove
BN41 1WR

Published in Australia
Crabtree Publishing
3 Charles Street
Coburg North
VIC 3058

CONTENTS

WIN THE DAY!

FOOTBALL STARDOM

Football players are tough! They get knocked down hard, stand up, dust themselves off, get back in the game…and then get pounded again. In addition to physical strength, the best of the best have a mental toughness that sets them apart. They are able to push themselves past the pain and fatigue to "leave it all on the field," meaning they do their best and give every ounce of energy they have each time they play. The legends in this book have given their hearts and souls to the sport of football, and they will be remembered forever by their fans.

> "If you're prepared, you're never scared."
> –Russell Wilson

Never Give Up

The road to pro football isn't easy for any player. Quarterback Russell Wilson had to fight even harder for his chance. Many teams thought that the 5'11" (1.8 m) athlete was too short to play in the NFL. He knew he could prove them wrong. In 2012, after being drafted by the Seattle Seahawks as the 75th overall pick, he tied Peyton Manning's 1998 record for most touchdown passes by a rookie (26). In his second season, he led the team to a Super Bowl victory.

Russell Wilson has the second-largest contract of any NFL quarterback, behind Aaron Rodgers. He signed a four-year deal in 2015 that is worth about $21.9 million per year.

Teamwork

Even the greatest football superstar could not win a game alone. Working as a team is one of the most important elements of the game.

Offense

For each play, there are 22 players on the field (11 from each team). If a team sends out too many players, it receives a penalty.

The team with possession of the ball plays offense. Their objective is to get the ball to the opponent's end zone to score points. The five offensive linemen (center, offensive guards, and offensive tackles) are responsible for blocking the other team's players—and protecting their own—during running and passing plays. The quarterback (QB) receives the ball from the center and calls plays. The QB has different options: running with the ball, handing it off to one of the running backs who will carry it forward, or throwing a pass to a receiver down the field.

Defense

When not in possession of the ball, a team's job is defense: to prevent their opponents from moving the ball forward and scoring. Defensive linemen (tackles and ends) start at the **line of scrimmage** and attempt to block the offensive line. This gives their linebackers, who are positioned behind them, a chance to take down the QB, running backs, or potential receivers. Defensive backs (cornerbacks and safety) start behind linebackers and try to prevent **wide receivers** from completing catches. They are also the defensive team's last hope to stop runners who make it to their zone.

FOOTBALL'S FIRST SUPERSTARS

Since the late 1800s, when football got its start on college campuses, it has become one of the most popular sports in North America. The rise in the sport's popularity began with the first superstars of football. Their mind-blowing moves showed spectators just how exciting the game could be.

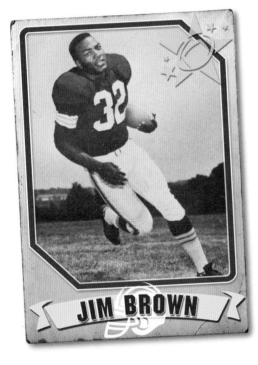

JIM BROWN

Jim Brown was known for being tough—he pushed for every yard he could get, was never afraid to be tackled, and he didn't go down easily.

Jim Brown

Hall-of-fame running back Jim Brown took the game to new heights. In 1957, his first season after being drafted by the Cleveland Browns, he led the league in **rushing yards** (942) and was named Rookie of the Year and league **MVP**. He went on to earn the MVP title three more times (1958, 1963, and 1965). He averaged over 100 yards per game and was the first player to make 100 **rushing** touchdowns. No matter how hard he was hit, Brown kept going. He didn't miss a single game or **Pro Bowl** in all of his nine seasons. When he retired at age 30 to pursue a career in acting, football fans were shocked and disappointed. Brown was gone from football, but he would never be forgotten.

Johnny Unitas

It's hard to believe that hall-of-fame QB Johnny Unitas wasn't always recognized as one of the best players on the **gridiron**. Even the Pittsburgh Steelers, who chose him in the ninth round of the 1955 draft, didn't know what they had. They cut him from the team before he ever played a game. "Johnny U" played **semipro** that season. The next year, the Baltimore Colts signed Unitas as a backup. When the starting QB got injured in the fourth game, Unitas—who would soon be known as "The Golden Arm"—came out to play. Over his 17 years with the team, the three-time league MVP went on to set many records, including making at least one touchdown pass in 47 consecutive games. The 1958 match in which Unitas helped the Colts beat the New York Giants in overtime has been called "the greatest game ever played."

Led by Johnny Unitas, the Colts won Super Bowl V (1970).

Dick Butkus

"There are no shortcuts and no magic carpet methods to success. It's nothing but hard work."
—*Johnny Unitas*

In his nine years as middle linebacker with the Chicago Bears, Dick Butkus developed a well-deserved reputation for playing hard that inspired fear in his opponents. Butkus was especially good at forcing fumbles. Other players were so wary of him that in 1970 *Sports Illustrated* featured him on its cover as "The Most Feared Man in the Game." The eight-time Pro Bowler made a career 1,020 tackles and was inducted into the hall of fame in 1979.

FIELD GENERALS

Quarterbacks are like generals leading an army. They have amazing **game sense**. They know the **playbook** inside and out, and can read the field to make split-second decisions about strategy. Superstar QBs are often recognized for their fast feet and powerful, accurate arms.

Joe Montana

Nicknamed "Joe Cool" for his ability to stay calm when he was losing, quarterback Joe Montana helped his team, the San Francisco 49ers, come from behind to win in the fourth quarter a mind-blowing 31 times. People called his power to pull off these exciting comebacks "Montana Magic." One of the most memorable moments took place in 1989 during Super Bowl XXIII against the Cincinnati Bengals. With his team losing by six points and less than a minute to go in the game, Montana drove the ball 92 yards for a winning touchdown. "The Comeback Kid" earned a total of four Super Bowl victories and was MVP in three of them. He retired with several career playoff records.

The 49ers drafted Joe Montana in 1979 and retired his number (16) in 1997. Montana was inducted into the hall of fame in 2000.

Peyton Manning

Peyton Manning's family tree has some footballs hanging on it. His father, Archie, was a pro quarterback and his brother, Eli, is QB for the New York Giants. Genetics may have played a role in Peyton's success, but hard work was the key. While getting an education at the University of Tennessee, Peyton tirelessly studied and memorized the playbook and **game film** to learn everything he could. In 1998, the Indianapolis Colts chose Peyton with the first overall draft pick. The QB with the cannon arm led the team to a win in Super Bowl XLI in 2007, and he took home game MVP. After 13 outstanding seasons with the Colts, Peyton had to miss the 2011 season while recovering from neck surgery, and was released from the team. Never one to give up, he signed with the Denver Broncos in 2012. He went on to be named Comeback Player of the Year, and set many team records. Peyton received his fifth league MVP award in 2013.

Peyton Manning broke the record for most career touchdown passes (509) in 2014.

CATCH THIS!

Drew Brees holds the NFL record for most consecutive games with a passing touchdown (54).

STATS

Born: 03/24/76
New Orleans, LA

Position: Quarterback
Height: 6 ft 5 in (1.96 m)

Team: #18 Denver Broncos

"Pressure is something you feel when you don't know what you're doing."
– Peyton Manning

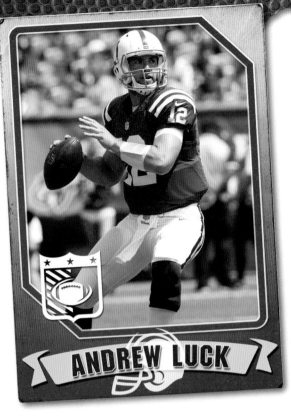

ANDREW LUCK

Andrew Luck was a finalist for the **Heisman Trophy** *in 2010 and 2011.*

STATS

Born: 09/12/89
Washington, D.C.

Position: Quarterback
Height: 6 ft 4 in (1.93 m)

Team: #12 Indianapolis Colts

Andrew Luck

Football is in Andrew Luck's blood. His father was a professional quarterback for the Houston Oilers before moving to Europe to manage football teams. Andrew's passion for football—and his raw talent—made him a standout player, even as a kid. By the time he reached high school, scouts had taken notice of him. He chose to attend Stanford University because he respected its academic program. While getting his degree in architecture, Luck built a name for himself in football. In 2012, he entered the NFL as the number one draft pick, and led the Indianapolis Colts to the playoffs in each of his first three seasons. Luck has broken many Colts **franchise** records, including most passing yards in a single season.

Quality Quarterbacks

- New England Patriots' Tom Brady spent most of his rookie season in 2000 on the bench as backup QB. When the team's starter was injured in 2001, Brady was able to show that he has one of the best arms in football. By 2015, Brady had earned four Super Bowl rings and had shattered many NFL records, including consecutive passes without an interception (358).

- The Canadian Football League's (CFL) Anthony Calvillo achieved more passing yards than any player in CFL history (79,816). He is one of only six pro QBs to have completed over 400 touchdown passes.

Aaron Rodgers

Rodgers was a star QB in high school, but he wasn't heavily recruited by the big football universities. He was patient. After playing for a year at community college, he transferred to the University of California, Berkeley, and was a Heisman finalist in 2004. His patience was tested again after the Green Bay Packers drafted him in 2005. In his first three seasons, he was backup QB to starter Brett Favre, and only played seven games. When Favre was traded in 2008, Rodgers finally got his chance. He helped lead the team to a Super Bowl XLV win in 2011 and was named league MVP. Rodgers isn't slowing down. He won his second NFL MVP award in 2014.

Aaron Rodgers has brawn and brains. He beat a famous astronaut and an entrepreneur to win the trivia quiz show "Celebrity Jeopardy!"

> "I'm fulfilling my dreams that I had as a kid every single day."
> – *Aaron Rodgers*

STATS

Born: 12/02/83
Chico, CA

Position: Quarterback
Height: 6 ft 2 in (1.88 m)

Team: #12 Green Bay Packers

- Hall-of-famer Dan Marino started his career off strong in 1983 as the NFL's Rookie of the Year for the Miami Dolphins. In his second season, he continued his domination as NFL MVP, setting six league records. By the end of his 17-year career, Marino was the passing leader in total attempts (8,358), completions (4,967), yards (61,361), and touchdowns (420).

- Sami Grisafe was the first female in California to play QB in a varsity Division I football game. Later she played women's tackle football for the Chicago Force and Team USA, where she helped her team to gold medal wins in the 2010 and 2013 **IFAF** Women's World Championships.

ACROBATIC WIDEOUTS

Wideouts have fast feet and good hands, meaning they can make unbelievable catches from the QB while running their play routes at track-star speed. The best of the best are focused, strong, and **agile**. They are able to anticipate plays and evade the best tacklers in the NFL by finding holes in their defense.

Jerry Rice

After being drafted by the San Francisco 49ers in 1985, Jerry Rice played 20 incredible seasons in the NFL. The wide receiver was known for his dedication to preparing his body and mind to be the best on the field. He worked hard and his efforts paid off. Rice holds almost every career receiving record in the NFL, including receptions (1,549), receiving yards (22,895), and total touchdowns (208). Not surprisingly, Rice was named NFL MVP in 1987 and was selected to the Pro Bowl 13 times. He brought home three Super Bowl rings (1988, 1989, and 1994) during his 15 years with the 49ers, and went on to share his skills with the Oakland Raiders and Seattle Seahawks before retiring.

Jerry Rice, who didn't start playing football until he was a sophomore in high school, was elected to the hall of fame in 2010.

Calvin Johnson

For proof that Calvin Johnson is a star football player, look no further than his picture on the cover of the *Madden NFL 13* video game, or his eight-year deal with the Detroit Lions worth up to $132 million, making him the highest paid wide receiver in the NFL. Johnson was one of the top draft picks in 2007. The two-time **All-American** at Georgia Tech wasn't a long shot. He performed amazingly well in the **Scouting Combine** and had the perfect stats to play with the best. At 6'5" (1.96 m) and 239 pounds (108 kg), he ran the 40-yard dash in 4.35 seconds. In 2012, Johnson broke three NFL records in one night: single season receiving yards (1,964), consecutive hundred yard games (eight), and consecutive games with 10 or more receptions (four). His amazing ability to run, leap, and catch makes him the franchise all-time leader in receiving yards and touchdowns. He is the best wide receiver the Detroit Lions have ever seen.

Johnson has played in five Pro Bowls.

CATCH THIS!

Randy Moss holds the NFL single-season touchdown reception record (23 in 2007).

STATS

Born: 09/29/85 Newnan, Georgia

Position: Wide receiver

Height: 6 ft 5 in (1.96 m)

Team: #81 Detroit Lions

13

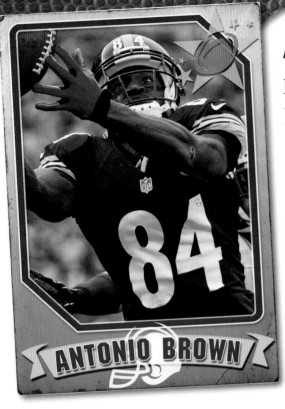

Antonio Brown was drafted 195th in 2010, but has proven that the Steelers made the right choice.

Antonio Brown

Pittsburgh Steelers' receiver Antonio Brown knows how to make an entrance. Whether he's driving up in his custom Steelers-themed Rolls-Royce Phantom (with its yellow stripe and his massive signature on the side) or rocking a Lego-themed haircut as he did in 2015, he makes sure that you can't miss him off the field. On the field, in full equipment, he gets noticed for his standout moves. In 2011, Brown became the first player in NFL history with at least 1,000 receiving yards (1,108) and at least 1,000 return yards (1,062) in the same season. In 2014, he was the NFL's receiving yards leader and reception leader. It's no surprise that Brown has been the Steelers MVP twice and has been named to three Pro Bowls.

STATS

Born: 07/10/88
Miami, Florida

Position: Wide receiver
Height: 5 ft 10 in (1.78 m)

Team: #84 Pittsburgh Steelers

Rocking Receivers

- The Dallas Cowboys' 2010 first-round draft pick Dez Bryant has proven his worth as a wide receiver. In 2014, he set the franchise record for receiving the most touchdowns in a single season (16).

- In 2011, Jordy Nelson made nine catches in Super Bowl XLV, helping to secure the Green Bay Packers' win against the Pittsburgh Steelers. He is one of the league leaders in receiving yards and touchdowns—and he still works on his family's farm during the off-season!

Rob Gronkowski

If Humpty Dumpty had the doctors, physiotherapists, and work ethic of New England Patriots' tight end Rob Gronkowski, he may actually have been put back together again. In the 2012 and 2013 seasons, "Gronk" had six surgeries after suffering several injuries: a herniated disk in his back, a broken left arm (twice), a concussion, and torn ligaments in his knee. This followed an amazing 2011 season, when the 6'6" (1.98 m), 265-pound (120 kg) receiver set records for most touchdown receptions (17) and most receiving yards (1,327) by a tight end in a season. Gronkowski worked hard to recover from his accidents, and he surprised doctors and fans by coming back strong. In 2014, after taking on defense players like they were made of paper, he was named Comeback Player of the Year. He even made a spectacular one-handed catch with the arm he had broken.

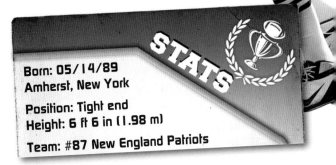

Born: 05/14/89 Amherst, New York

Position: Tight end
Height: 6 ft 6 in (1.98 m)

Team: #87 New England Patriots

Gronk was a key part of the Patriots' exciting win at Super Bowl XLIX (2014).

● Since 2010, three-time Pro Bowler Demaryius Thomas has set franchise records for the Denver Broncos, including most receiving yards in a season (1,619 in 2014). He also holds the record for most receptions in a Super Bowl, with 13 during the 2013 championship.

● During Geroy Simon's 15 seasons as a **slotback** in the CFL, 12 of which he spent with the BC Lions, he was named to the All-Star team six times, won three **Grey Cup** championships, and was named the league's Most Outstanding Player in 2006.

LEADING RUSHERS

The best NFL players in this position use more than one weapon against defenders while carrying the ball down the field—speed to outrun them, agility to avoid them, and strength to break a tackle. Superstar running backs have the game vision to find a hole in the defense, and they can get there fast.

Walter 'Sweetness' Payton

The Chicago Bears' first-round draft pick in 1975 has inspired all running backs that have come after him. The hall-of-famer's creative moves, including the "stutter-step" run that he developed in order to confuse tacklers, made him a force on the field. He was also recognized for his speed, strength, agility (at times he leapt over his opponents!), and courage. His determination on the gridiron won him many NFL records over his 13 seasons with the Bears, including the single game rushing record of 275 yards. Payton was a Super Bowl Champ (XX, 1985), two-time NFL MVP, and nine-time Pro Bowler.

"Never die easy."
– Walter S Payton

During his life, Walter Payton worked tirelessly for many charities. Now, the Walter Payton NFL Man of the Year Award honors a player for their community service.

Marshawn Lynch

They call Marshawn Lynch "Beast Mode." He is known for besting would-be defenders by avoiding them…or running through them. In 2014, Lynch broke 101 tackles. He is relentless and often continues to gain yards even after contact.

Surprisingly, Lynch's career started off rough. After being drafted by the Buffalo Bills in 2007, he didn't play as well as expected. In 2010, Lynch was traded to the Seattle Seahawks. He started out with some fumbles, but things began to turn around and Lynch was trusted with over 23 carries per game by the end of 2011. Now, Beast Mode is an NFL rushing yards leader, five-time Pro Bowler, and a Super Bowl Champion (XLVIII, 2014).

STATS

Born: 04/22/86 Oakland, California

Position: Running back

Height: 5 ft 11 in (1.80 m)

Team: #24 Seattle Seahawks

Marshawn Lynch helps at-risk youth through his foundation in Oakland, California.

17

DeMarco Murray

DeMarco Murray was the NFL's top rusher, setting a franchise record for the Dallas Cowboys in 2014 (1,845 yards). This was outstanding, considering he was only drafted 71st in 2011. He has also beaten the record for most games with over 100 rushing yards in a season (12), and most single game rushing yards (253). The Cowboys trusted Murray enough to hand him the ball 392 times in 2014. That's why, in 2015, it came as a huge surprise (and disappointment) to many of his fans and teammates when Murray signed a five-year $42-million deal with the Philadelphia Eagles. Murray's first year with the Eagles started out poorly. Hopefully, he will get his groove back.

DeMarco Murray beat other running backs by over 500 yards to earn the 2014 rushing title.

STATS

Born: 02/12/88
Las Vegas, Nevada
Position: Running back
Height: 6 ft 0 in (1.83 m)
Team: #29 Philadelphia Eagles

Remarkable Running Backs

- The Dallas Cowboys made a great pick when they chose Emmitt Smith in 1990. He helped the team to three Super Bowl Championships (1993, 1994, and 1996) and took home the Super Bowl MVP and NFL MVP awards in 1993. Smith was inducted into the hall of fame in 2010.

- Hall-of-famer Barry Sanders proved his special skills during his 10 seasons with the Detroit Lions (1989-1998). He holds the NFL record for consecutive seasons with over 1,000 yards rushing (10). In 2013, he was chosen by fans to appear on the cover of the popular video game *Madden NFL 25*.

Jamaal Charles

Jamaal Charles is used to working hard and not giving up. At the University of Texas, he proved that he could excel academically despite his learning disabilities. He had an uphill battle when he joined the NFL, too. During his rookie season, the Kansas City Chiefs barely used him (he rushed only 67 times). In 2009, the coach even listed Charles as inactive during a game when he was healthy. But, he showed them his worth. During each of the last four games that year, he rushed for 100 yards. Now, he's a four-time Pro Bowler, the Chiefs' rushing yards career leader, and the NFL career leader in average yards per carry (5.5). He has won more Derrick Thomas Awards for being MVP of the Chiefs than any other player on the team.

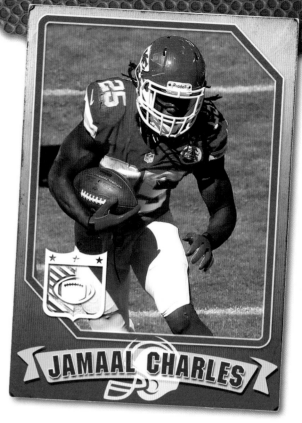

Each year, Jamaal Charles gives scholarships to five University of Texas students with learning disabilities.

STATS

Born: 12/27/86
Port Arthur, Texas

Position: Running back
Height: 5 ft 11 in (1.80 m)

Team: #25 Kansas City Chiefs

Right after being drafted second overall by the Los Angeles Rams in 1983, Eric Dickerson become the Rookie of the Year and eventually became the first player to gain more than 1,000 yards in seven consecutive seasons.

Michael "Pinball" Clemons (CFL) signed with the Toronto Argonauts in 1989. Before he retired in 2000, he racked up 12 all-time team records, including the pro football record for most combined yards in a career (25,438). He also won three Grey Cup championships as a player, and one as head coach for the team (in 2004).

STRONGMAN LINE

Offensive linemen (guards, tackles, and center) are responsible for blocking for the QB and running backs, and creating holes in the opposition's defense so that pass plays and running plays can succeed. Defensive linemen (tackles and ends) stop the offense from blocking. They also tackle runners and try to take down the QB. Both offensive and defensive linemen are tough and big. Despite their size, they are also agile and fast on their feet.

Joe Thomas

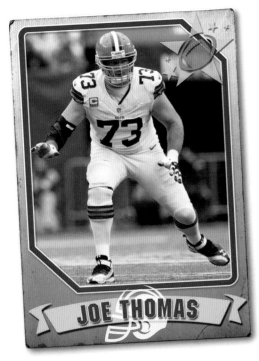

JOE THOMAS

When Joe Thomas was up for the draft in 2007, he chose not to attend the event. He spent the day fishing with his dad on Lake Michigan instead. While catching trout, he also managed to reel in a spot as offensive tackle with the Cleveland Browns. By 2014, Thomas had been named to the Pro Bowl every year since he joined the league. Thomas has been on the line for 7,917 consecutive **snaps** since the start of his rookie season—and he's still going strong.

Joe Thomas is an amazing all-around athlete. In high school, he lettered in football, track, and basketball.

STATS

Born: 12/04/84
Brookfield, Wisconsin

Position: Offensive tackle

Height: 6 ft 6 in (1.98 m)

Team: #73 Cleveland Browns

J. J. Watt

Quarterbacks are right to worry when they see J. J. Watt standing on the opposite side of the line of scrimmage. The 2011 first-round draft pick for the Houston Texans is one of the top defensive ends in the league. In 2014, the 6'5" (1.96 m), 289-pound (131 kg) lineman became the first NFL player to complete a second season with more than 20 **sacks**. He also holds the Texans' record for **forced fumbles**. Not only does Watt prevent points, but he also earns them. Watt is known for **picking off** passes and returning for a touchdown (TD). He scored five TDs in 2014 alone. Watt is one of the highest paid non-quarterbacks in the NFL. The playmaker is worth every penny.

J.J. Watt showed his stuff during the 2011 Scouting Combine by performing a 37-inch (94 cm) vertical jump.

CATCH THIS!

Defensive end Bruce Smith holds the NFL career record for quarterback sacks with an impressive 200 during his 19 seasons. J.J. Watt is currently at 60 in his fifth season.

STATS

Born: 03/22/89
Waukesha, Wisconsin

Position: Defensive end
Height: 6 ft 5 in (1.96 m)

Team: #99 Houston Texans

AGILE LINEBACKERS

You wouldn't want to mess with an athlete who plays this position. Running into one would feel a bit like hitting a brick wall. Not only are they strong, but the best linebackers can also quickly read the opposition's offense and direct the defensive play.

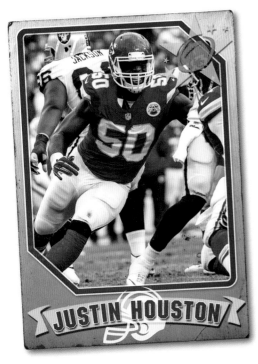

Justin Houston was only a sack away from beating Michael Strahan's single-season NFL record (22.5 sacks in 2001).

Justin Houston

Looking back, it's clear that scouts underestimated Justin Houston's talent. It took until the third round of the 2011 draft for a team to call his name. While he had to wait for 69 players to be drafted ahead of him, it didn't take long for the Kansas City Chiefs to realize that they had signed one of the hardest-working players—and best defensemen—in the league. Once they had him, they didn't want to let him go. Houston's six-year contract extension worth $101 million makes him the highest paid linebacker in NFL history. In 2014, he was the NFL sacks leader with 22, which set a franchise single season record, and won him the Deacon Jones Award for the player with the most QB sacks.

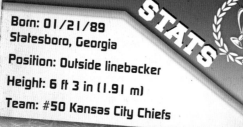

STATS

Born: 01/21/89
Statesboro, Georgia
Position: Outside linebacker
Height: 6 ft 3 in (1.91 m)
Team: #50 Kansas City Chiefs

Luke Kuechly

Luke Kuechly started to play football in fourth grade, and he's still finding ways to develop his game. He doesn't have much room for improvement. In 2014, he led the NFL in tackles, was named Defensive Player of the Year, and won the Butkus Award for top linebacker in the league. Kuechly's high school and college coaches wouldn't be surprised by his success. He has always had an amazing instinct for the game, and great **pass coverage** ability. Kuechly broke several **NCAA** tackling records before he went pro. After being drafted in 2012 by the Carolina Panthers, he proved to be a star right out of the gate, and was named AP Defensive Rookie of the Year.

Kuechly performed well during the Scouting Combine and was the first linebacker selected for the 2012 draft.

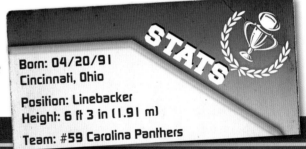

STATS

Born: 04/20/91
Cincinnati, Ohio

Position: Linebacker
Height: 6 ft 3 in (1.91 m)

Team: #59 Carolina Panthers

Legendary Linebackers

- New York Giants' Lawrence Taylor dominated from the moment he stepped onto the gridiron as a rookie in 1981. The hall-of-fame tackler won NFL MVP in 1986 and played in ten Pro Bowls. Taylor helped his team to Super Bowl championships in 1987 and 1991 (XXL, XXV).

- Green Bay Packers' Clay "CM3" Matthews III has tackling in his blood. His grandfather, father, uncle, cousins, and brother have all played in the NFL. While his job alone may not provide bragging rights in the Matthews family, at least CM3 gets to show off his 2011 Super Bowl ring (XLV) and the Butkus Award he took home in 2010 for being the top linebacker in the league.

23

SECONDARY STARS

The four or five players in the defensive backfield (DB), also known as "the secondary," protect against passing or rushing plays. Superstars in this position can predict offensive plays, and then quickly get to where they need to be. When the best DBs are on the field, opponents avoid their zone for fear of getting shut down.

Richard Sherman

The Seattle Seahawks chose Richard Sherman as the 154th pick in 2011. Not being drafted until the fifth day was devastating for Sherman, who was used to being the best at anything he did. He was a football and track star in high school, and graduated with a 4.2 grade point average. At Stanford University he excelled again. The player who scouts said lacked instinct and speed was the NFL interceptions leader in 2013, and helped the Seahawks win their first Super Bowl in 2014 with a 43-8 win over the Denver Broncos.

The Seattle Seahawks defensive backfield is referred to as "The Legion of Boom."

"I like every aspect of defense; I enjoy shutting down the offense."
– *Richard Sherman*

24

STATS

Born: 03/30/88
Compton, California
Position: Cornerback
Height: 6 ft 3 in (1.91 m)
Team: #25 Seattle Seahawks

Darrelle Revis

New York Jets' cornerback Darrelle Revis names the area that he is defending on the gridiron "Revis Island," because opposing receivers often get stranded there without a ball ever thrown their way. Quarterbacks avoid throwing to his zone for good reason. Since 2007, Revis has racked up 400 tackles, two sacks, 24 interceptions, and 124 passes defended. The 2015 Super Bowl champ (XLIX) is skilled at reading the offense, and he doesn't wait for the opposing team to make their move. He takes control. Off the field, he is quiet but equally gutsy. The six-time Pro Bowler (who has also played for the Tampa Bay Buccaneers and New England Patriots) negotiated one of the best contracts in the league, and is currently the highest-paid cornerback in the NFL.

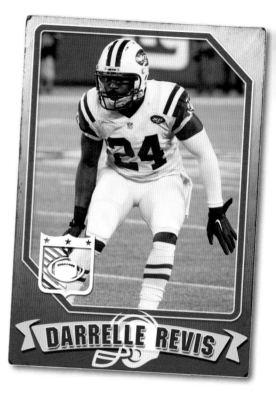

Darrelle Revis was picked 14th in the first round of the 2007 NFL draft.

STATS

Born: 07/14/85
Aliquippa, Pennsylvania

Position: Cornerback
Height: 5 ft 11 in (1.80 m)

Team: # 24 New York Jets

Dangerous Defensive Backs

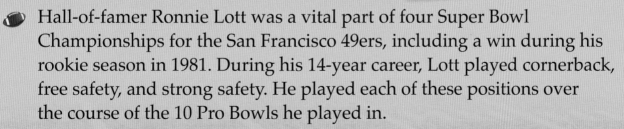

- Hall-of-famer Ronnie Lott was a vital part of four Super Bowl Championships for the San Francisco 49ers, including a win during his rookie season in 1981. During his 14-year career, Lott played cornerback, free safety, and strong safety. He played each of these positions over the course of the 10 Pro Bowls he played in.

- Roland "Champ" Bailey recently retired after 15 seasons in the NFL. He made his mark while playing for the Washington Redskins and Denver Broncos. Bailey was selected to play in 12 Pro Bowls, which is more than any cornerback in history.

Some of the most important people in a football game never suit up in pads and helmets. Superstar coaches and referees are game changers who inspire fans and players by being the best at what they do.

Vince Lombardi was on his way to turning around the Washington Redskins, just as he had the Packers, when he passed away suddenly in 1970. His name is now on the trophy given to the Super Bowl champion each year.

> "It's not whether you get knocked down, it's whether you get up."
> – *Vince Lombardi*

Vince Lombardi, Coach

There are 53 players on an NFL **roster**, but Vince Lombardi proved that just one good coach can mean the difference between winning and losing for a team. After five years as assistant coach with the New York Giants, Lombardi became the head coach for the Green Bay Packers. In the 1960's NFL, he turned the team from an underdog into a force to be reckoned with. With Lombardi in charge, the team won five NFL championships and Super Bowls I and II (1967 and 1968). He worked hard and expected no less from his players. They had good reason to listen to him. His record of 105 wins, 35 losses, and six ties in the NFL spoke for itself. He was elected into the hall of fame in 1971, and will be remembered as one of the greatest football coaches of all time.

Pete Carroll, Coach

He's not your typical drill sergeant of a football coach. He earns players' respect and inspires them to follow his lead. His unique approach to coaching hasn't always been appreciated by NFL management. Carroll was fired from both the New York Jets and the New England Patriots. He kept coaching, but moved from the pros to the University of Southern California from 2000 to 2009. There, his team earned seven straight **Pac-10** titles and two national championships. In 2010, Carroll tried the NFL again as head coach and executive vice president of the Seattle Seahawks. In 2014, he led the team to their first Super Bowl victory in franchise history.

As a coach, Pete Carroll has won both a College Football National Championship and a Super Bowl.

Ed Hochuli, Referee

Ed Hochuli is a busy man. Not only does he have his day job as a lawyer, but he also refs NFL games on the side. He's used to the pace. He has been a league ref since 1990. While most members of the crew in the striped jerseys remain anonymous, people know Hochuli by name. In fact, his

Ed Hochuli has worked two Super Bowls.

character is even featured in the *Madden NFL* video games. Hochuli became famous for the long explanations he gives when he makes a call. People also know him for his bulking biceps. He has been nicknamed "Hochules" (like Hercules) because of his physique.

RISING SUPERSTARS

Even people who don't follow football know the names of standout players like Peyton Manning and Tom Brady. The athletes on these pages have it in them to become the next big stars of the gridiron.

Odell Beckham Jr.

The wide receiver for the New York Giants is the youngest player to ever make it to the cover of a *Madden NFL* video game. Beckham Jr. beat out tough competition, including Rob Gronkowski, for the cover, which proves what an amazing year he had. In 2014, he was named Offensive Rookie of the Year. Even though he missed the first several games because of an injury, he broke numerous New York Giants' rookie records, including most receiving yards (1,305) and most receptions (91). He also smashed NFL records, including fastest player to reach 100 career receptions (14 games). The feat most football fans will remember about Beckham Jr.'s 2014 year is the one-handed touchdown reception that he made during a game against the Dallas Cowboys.

The jersey that Odell Beckham Jr. wore during his one-handed catch is on display in the hall of fame.

STATS

Born: 11/05/92
Baton Rouge, Louisiana
Position: Wide receiver
Height 5 ft 11 in (1.80 m)
Team #13 New York Giants

Aaron Donald

When the St. Louis Rams selected Aaron Donald in the first round of the 2014 draft, they did well. The tackle was named 2014 Defensive Rookie of the Year and was selected to the 2015 Pro Bowl. In college, Donald won every major award that a defensive lineman possibly could. He was also a standout player at the Scouting Combine. In his first year, Donald was the rookie league leader in sacks (nine) and finished with 72 tackles.

STATS

Born: 05/23/91
Pittsburgh, Pennsylvania

Position: Defensive tackle
Height 6 ft 1 in (1.85 m)

Team: #99 St. Louis Rams

Aaron Donald was off to a good start in 2015. He was the first National Football Conference (NFC) Defensive Player of the Week.

Teddy Bridgewater joined the team after being selected 32nd in the draft—the final pick of the first round.

Teddy Bridgewater

Teddy Bridgewater, quarterback for the Minnesota Vikings, had to hang on for some time before he got his chance to play. Bridgewater was second QB to starter Matt Cassel. When Cassel broke his foot during a game, the rookie stepped up. He went on to break almost all Minnesota Vikings records for a rookie QB.

The outstanding athlete was chosen by fans as the Pepsi NFL Rookie of the Year for 2014, and was quarterback of the NFL All-Rookie team.

STATS

Born: 11/10/92
Miami, Florida

Position: Quarterback
Height 6 ft 2 in (1.88 m)

Team: #5 Minnesota Vikings

Women play competitive tackle football, too. If you didn't know that already, it's probably because the sport doesn't receive the same respect or publicity that the men's game gets. Women don't get paid the sky-high salaries that male players do and, in fact, have to pay to play. The athletes in the Independent Women's Football League (IWFL), the Women's Spring Football League (WSFL), and the Women's Football Alliance (WFA) are all working hard to change that.

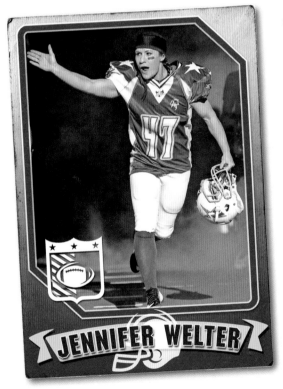

"I knew it was opening doors for all my sisters. It's something bigger than yourself that makes it so great."
– *Jennifer Welter*

Jennifer Welter

Jennifer Welter is blazing trails for women in pro football. In the summer of 2015, she became the first woman to coach in the NFL, as a preseason trainee with the Arizona Cardinals. She brought plenty of experience along. In 2014 she became the first female running back on a men's pro team by joining the Texas Revolution in the Champions Indoor Football League. In February 2015, the Revolution made her their linebackers and special teams coach. This made her the first woman to coach in any men's pro league. She earlier played women's football and college rugby.

LEARNING MORE

Can't get enough of football's amazing superstars? Check out these books, websites, and videos for more information.

Books

Big Book of Who: Football, Revised & Updated by editors of Sports Illustrated for Kids, c. 2015, Sports Illustrated

The Everything Kids' Football Book, 4th Edition by Greg Jacobs, c. 2014, Adams Media

Football Superstars 2015 by K.C. Kelley, c. 2015, Scholastic

Websites

The National Football League's Official Site
www.nfl.com

This site features NFL standings as well as information on teams and players. Click on the video link "Can't Miss Plays" and watch the league's biggest stars make moves you have to see to believe.

Pro Football Hall-of-Fame
www.profootballhof.com

The Pro Football Hall-of-Fame has information about the history of football and the best football players of the past.

GLOSSARY

agile Being able to move quickly and easily

All-American Selected as one of the best in the U.S.

forced fumble A forced fumble occurs when the ball carrier loses the football due to the force of a defensive player. This can be a result of being hit or of having the ball stripped by a defender.

franchise A team that is a member of a professional sports league

game film Videos of past games. Players can watch their own team or the opposing team and adjust strategy.

game sense A deep or instinctive understanding of the game

Grey Cup The championship game of the Canadian Football League (CFL)

gridiron A term for the football field. It was named for the original pattern of parallel lines on the grass, which was thought to resemble a gridiron, which is a metal grate used for grilling meat over an open fire.

Heisman Trophy The award given to the most outstanding player in college football

IFAF International Federation of American Football

Line of scrimmage An imaginary line in football that marks the position of the ball at the start of each down

MVP Most Valuable Player award

NCAA National Collegiate Athletic Association

Pac-10 A collegiate athletic conference

pass coverage Efforts of the defense to stop the opposing team from completing a forward pass

playbook A book that contains descriptions of the different offensive and defensive plays that are used by a team

Pro Bowl The all-star game of the National Football League (NFL)

roster The official list of players on the team

rushing To advance the ball while running with it

rushing yards The total number of yards gained by a single player as the result of a rushing play (or plays), in which the player carries the football (as opposed to receiving a pass)

sack When the quarterback (or another offensive player acting as a passer) is tackled behind the line of scrimmage before he can throw a forward pass

Scouting Combine An event where the best college players are invited to perform/try out in front of NFL coaches, scouts, and managers.

semipro An athlete for whom sport is not a full-time occupation

slotback An offensive football halfback who lines up just behind the slot between an offensive end and tackle

snap The backward passing of the ball inward, at the start of play from scrimmage

wide receiver An offensive player who is positioned at a distance from the end and is used primarily as a pass receiver

INDEX

32